Understanding Self-Image and Confidence

Toney Allman

San Diego, CA

For more information, contact:
ReferencePoint Press, Inc.
PO Box 27779
San Diego, CA 92198
www.ReferencePointPress.com

LIBRARY OF CONGRESS CATALOGING-IN-PUBLICATION DATA

Name: Allman, Toney, author.
Title: Understanding Self-Image and Confidence/by Toney Allman.
Description: San Diego, CA: ReferencePoint Press, Inc., [2018] | Series: Understanding psychology | Includes bibliographical references and index. | Description based on print version record and CIP data provided by publisher.
Identifiers: LCCN 2017021325 (print) | LCCN 2017029674 (ebook) | ISBN 9781682822807 (eBook) | ISBN 9781682822791 (hardback)
Subjects: LCSH: Self-perception in adolescence—Juvenile literature. | Self-esteem in adolescence—Juvenile literature. | Self-confidence in adolescence—Juvenile literature.
Classification: LCC BF697.5.S43 (ebook) | LCC BF697.5.S43 A445 2018 (print) | DDC 155.2—dc23
LC record available at https://lccn.loc.gov/2017021325

CONTENTS

The Human Brain: Thought,
Behavior, and Emotion   4

Introduction   5
What Is Self-Image?

Chapter One   9
How Does Self-Image Develop?

Chapter Two   20
Positive Self-Image and High Self-Esteem

Chapter Three   32
Negative Self-Image and Low Self-Esteem

Chapter Four   44
What About Body Image?

Chapter Five   56
Can Self-Image Be Improved?

Source Notes   68

For Further Research   72

Index   74

Picture Credits   79

About the Author   80

The Human Brain: Thought, Behavior, and Emotion

Frontal lobe controls:
- Thinking
- Planning
- Organizing
- Problem solving
- Short-term memory
- Movement
- Personality
- Emotions
- Behavior
- Language

Parietal lobe:
- Interprets sensory information such as taste, temperature, and touch

Temporal lobe:
- Processes information from the senses of smell, taste, and hearing
- Plays role in memory storage

Occipital lobe:
- Processes images from the eyes
- Links information with images stored in memory

Source: Mayo Foundation for Education and Research, "Slide Show: How Your Brain Works." www.mayoclinic.org.

INTRODUCTION

What Is Self-Image?

Self-image is the mental picture that each person has of himself or herself. It consists of how people think about themselves and what internal pictures and words they use to describe themselves. This internal concept of self is built up over a lifetime of personal experiences, learning, and social interactions. Psychologists explain that a person's self-image is the product of the thinking self; it is the way each individual organizes all the facts about himself or herself that have been acquired over the years. However, all the facets of one's self-image may or may not be accurate. For instance, a young man with a birthmark on his face may decide that the mark is the dominant feature of his appearance, while in reality the mark may be so pale that other people do not notice it upon first meeting him. Self-image is influenced by external events (such as how others relate to a person), but it is an internal belief system that may not coincide with the reality that other people perceive.

The Aspects of Self-Image

Each person's self-image includes three major components: a physical description, social roles, and personality traits. The physical description of each person's self-image includes ideas such as "I have brown hair," "I am tall," and "I am overweight." Physical components of self-image are important because they help define a person as a unique individual and because people know that others often form initial impressions of them based on appearance. Social roles are the ties people have to social groups that are important to them. Social groups and ties give people a sense of social identity. These may include relationships, career choices, friendship patterns, religious affiliations, or anything else that gives people a feeling of membership in a larger group. Examples of social roles by which people define self-image are "I am the father of the Jones family," "I am Catholic," "I am a soldier," and "I am a high school student."

Finally, personality traits are the enduring characteristics that define each person's unique patterns of responding to the world and to society. The personality traits by which people define themselves vary with each individual. For example, a person may say, "I am stubborn," "I am friendly," "I am shy," or "I love partying." Many different personality traits are incorporated into each person's self-image.

Every person's self-image is complex and dynamic, meaning it changes with new experiences. The things people believe about themselves are so varied that social psychologists often refer to self-schemas instead of one unified self-image. Social psychologist Roy F. Baumeister explains that a schema is "an individual piece of information or a specific belief about the self."[1] This means that people may describe themselves differently in different situations or when faced with different social interactions, depending on the schema that seems most pertinent at the time. For instance, in one social setting a person may define himself or herself as shy, while in another, intimate situation, he or she may think in terms of empathy or talkativeness. Nevertheless, people are usually conscious of an overall concept of themselves as whole beings with stable traits that define who they are.

WORDS IN CONTEXT

schema

A mental concept about a specific piece of information or aspect of self.

Self-Esteem and the Ideal Self

Any one aspect of the self-image may be accurate or inaccurate, and a person may view each schema of the self-image as posi-

Self-image is the mental picture that a person has of himself or herself. Social interaction is one of the primary ways that an individual develops this mental picture.

tive, negative, or anywhere in between. An individual may know, for instance, that he or she is shy and also feel that shyness is a negative trait. The same individual, however, may also see himself or herself as an intelligent student who earns good grades and deem that aspect of self as positive. How people feel about their self-image as a whole determines self-esteem. Self-esteem grows from an evaluation of self-image and is a description of how much people like or approve of their self-image. Self-esteem is the feeling self as opposed to the thinking, or cognitive, self that defines self-image.

Much of one's judgment about self-image is based on comparing the self-image to one's ideal self. The ideal self is the person each individual wishes to be. The ideal self is shaped by a person's experiences, family expectations, reactions of peers, social demands and values, and even the media. The feeling self compares knowledge of self-image to the mental picture of the ideal self. When ideal self and self-image are too different, the feeling self makes a negative judgment about the self-image. Self-esteem suffers when the feeling self evaluates self-image and finds it to be of lacking in value and perhaps unworthy. People with a poor self-image, in which most schemas are thought of negatively, may have low self-esteem. Conversely, when the self-image is mostly positive, people enjoy a high level of self-esteem. They feel good about themselves most of the time, have confidence in themselves, and feel acceptable and accepted in social situations. How people feel about their self-image, then, is what makes understanding self-image so important.

The Significance of Self

Social psychology is the branch of psychology that deals with social interactions and how they affect individuals. Social psychologists view concepts of self and the ways people see and evaluate themselves as the foundation of all human behavior. As social psychologists Roy F. Baumeister and Brad Bushman explain, "People are built to relate to other people. Even the 'self,' much discussed and invoked throughout social psychology, is designed to cultivate social acceptance and other forms of success that are valued in human cultures."[2] Social psychologists devote a lot of research to understanding how a sense of self develops, how people think and feel about self, how society affects the sense of self, and how people might overcome problems related to self-image, self-esteem, and self-confidence.

CHAPTER 1

How Does Self-Image Develop?

No one is born with a sense of self. Developing a self-image is a lifelong process that begins at birth. Psychologists have determined a series of regular stages that everyone goes through as the concept of self emerges, and self-image becomes more complex with life experiences.

Born Ready

Babies are born with a rudimentary body awareness that is the beginning of self-awareness. From their earliest hours, they are able to distinguish between their own bodies and the bodies of others. In other words, they understand that their bodies are their own and not a part of the general environment. They also are able to use their bodies purposefully to obtain something they want. In one famous study, for example, Anthony J. DeCasper and William P. Fifer demonstrated that infants less than two days old would suck harder on a pacifier in order to hear a recording of their mother's voice as opposed to a stranger's voice. This experiment proved not only that infants bond with their mothers from an early age but also that they have some sense of their own bodies (their mouths) as separate from the rest of the environment and that they can use their bodies to effect a change in their worlds.

Using their senses, infants become body aware. They learn to move their body parts at will and to explore the environment with their mouth, eyes, ears, nose, and sense of touch. Socially, self-awareness begins to develop at about two months of age, when babies begin to smile, coo, and make eye contact with another person (usually the mother). At this time, the infant has the beginnings of self-knowledge. Psychologists know that these behaviors represent self-knowledge because of several studies of babies' social interactions. These studies involve people suddenly freezing their facial expressions and refusing to smile back at the infants. Babies respond dramatically negatively to those blank expressions. They refuse to look at the person's face, stop smiling, and often cry. Psychologist Philippe Rochat says, "This robust phenomenon suggests that infants already have an implicit sense of others, as well as of themselves, as reciprocating (social) agents. They expect social partners to reciprocate in certain ways to their own emotional displays."[3]

Nevertheless, in the first few months of life, infants have only basic, simple (or implicit) self-knowledge. They do not yet have an explicit concept of themselves. Their reactions depend on action (reaching for an object because they know their hands are part of their bodies and that objects are outside their bodies) and their senses. Explicit self-awareness is different: It depends on learning and experience and is expressed in terms of "I" or "me" as a distinct individual. It includes specific self-schemas about the body and about how other people relate to the infant. This concept of self slowly develops as babies learn about their environment and other people. Around five months of age, for instance, infants truly understand that they are separate being from their mothers. Babies learn to respond to their own names and to prefer familiar caretakers to strangers. They are becoming social beings who are aware of positive interactions with other "selves." Not until about eighteen months of age, however, do infants demonstrate an explicit concept of themselves by recognizing themselves in a mirror.

> **WORDS IN CONTEXT**
>
> **implicit**
> Automatic or unconscious; not requiring conscious thought.
>
> **explicit**
> Conscious; deliberately formed and remembered.

Me in the Mirror

In the development of a concept of self and the growth of self-image, mirror recognition is a very important milestone. It is not

just body awareness. The mirror image is a reflection and symbol of the self. It cannot be recognized as self until an infant has his or her own mental concept of self. Mirror recognition has been tested by psychologists in many studies. Generally, the experimenter surreptitiously places something on a part of the baby that he or she cannot see. It may be a spot of blush dabbed on the baby's nose or cheek or a Post-it note or sticker stuck on the top of the baby's head. Babies who recognize the image in the mirror will react by reaching for the mark or paper or by touching their head or nose to see what is there. Often, the babies try to rub off the mark or remove the sticker. Some babies even act ashamed or embarrassed, as if they know that other people have observed their abnormal, inappropriate appearance. Self-image seems to be inextricably tied to awareness of others, caring about what others think, and becoming a social being.

Gordon G. Gallup Jr. has been studying self-awareness and social awareness for many years. He explains:

> If . . . an organism that can recognize itself is one that can also conceive of itself, this opens up some extraordinary possibilities. Once you are aware of yourself, and therefore are aware of being aware, you find yourself in the unique position of being able to use your experience as a means of modeling the experience of others. . . . Knowledge of self, in other words, paves the way for an intuitive knowledge of others.[4]

This is why self-image seems to develop as a result of interactions with other people. Children incorporate the reactions of others into their own self-images. The younger the child, the more crucial are the opinions and reactions of parents or primary caretakers. Loving, approving parents are the most important others in the development of any young child's self-image.

Growing into Childhood

Throughout their preschool years, children acquire information about themselves through the eyes of other people and build their own concepts about themselves. These basic pieces of self-image include age, whether they are boys or girls, and an ability to describe some of their physical characteristics, such as eye or hair color. By age six most children can use the reactions of others to conceive of their own traits and to think about their own behaviors as distinct to themselves. Their self-image is not just descriptive, but also evaluative and judgmental. This means that they understand that other people look at them and judge them and that they look at and judge others. They know that others form a mental picture of them, just as they have mental pictures of other people.

Do Animals Have Self-Awareness?

Gordon G. Gallup Jr. developed the mirror recognition test for studying self-awareness in 1970 to find out whether nonhuman animals could recognize themselves in a mirror. Since that time many animals (and human children) have been tested to see whether they touch a mark placed on their own body that they can see only by looking in a mirror. Using the mirror recognition test, researchers have discovered that some animals, such as dogs and cats, never seem to realize that the animal in the mirror is a reflection of themselves. However, at least some animals do have self-awareness and pass the mirror test. These animals are chimpanzees, bonobos, elephants, orangutans, bottlenose dolphins, orca whales, and European magpies. Some gorillas pass the test, although most do not. Scientists speculate that in some cases the mirror does not accurately reflect self-awareness. Gorillas, for instance, may be self-aware, but since they do not look at each other's faces and eyes because such looking is aggressive, perhaps they do not look in the mirror long enough to recognize themselves. Rhesus monkeys do not recognize themselves in mirrors naturally, but in 2017 one group of researchers in Shanghai spent weeks training three rhesus monkeys to understand how to use a mirror. After that, the monkeys easily passed the mirror recognition test by pawing at the marks the scientists had placed on their cheeks. Although most scientists believe that self-awareness is rare among animals, the Shanghai researchers wonder whether it is more common than people think.

These evaluations are based on mental and emotional behaviors, as well as physical traits. The opinions of schoolmates, teachers, extended family members, and friends become more and more important during the grade school years, and the judgments of parents (although still important) begin to become less significant. When asked to describe themselves, children in this age range are able to say things like "I am a nice person" or "I am smart." They may describe abilities, such as being a good student or being good at sports. They compare themselves to peers and know whether they are taller or shorter than their friends or popular or shy. They also have feelings about the schemas of their self-image.

As children move through grade school, the opinions of friends and those outside their immediate family become more important to them as the influence of parents diminishes.

All children develop positive and negative feelings about self-image, based on their judgments of themselves and on how they perceive others judge them. By age five, psychologists say, self-esteem is established, based on the child's overall perceptions about self. Five-year-olds are not yet able to put into words their good or bad feelings about themselves as people. But social psychologists can explore children's levels of self-esteem with carefully constructed studies. Psychologist Dario Cvencek and his team at the University of Washington published the results of one such study in 2016. The researchers taught 234 five-year-olds to play a matching game with small flags that were labeled "me" and "not me." Then the children listened to a series of good words and bad words and pushed buttons on a computer to choose a flag for each word. Good words included *fun*, *happy*, *good*, and *nice*. Bad words were terms like *yucky*, *bad*, and *mean*. The research team used the results to measure how positively the children felt about themselves. Most of the children chose flags that showed they thought of themselves as more good than bad. They had high self-esteem. Anthony Greenwald, a member of the team, concludes, "Previously we understood that preschoolers knew about some of their specific good features. We now understand that, in addition, they have a global, overall knowledge of their goodness as a person."[5]

The researchers also discovered through further studies that children with high self-esteem had strong gender identities (feeling comfortable with their gender) and strongly preferred being with and playing with children of the same sex. Cvencek suggests that this association indicates that social roles

WORDS IN CONTEXT

perception
The recognition and interpretation of stimuli from the senses.

and the level of confidence a child feels in a social group are related to self-esteem. He says, "Self-esteem appears to play a critical role in how children form various social identities."[6] His research team plans to follow the children as they grow older to see how much self-image and self-esteem change and what experiences are most important for maintaining high self-esteem.

Self-Image and Adolescence

Other psychologists have been able to describe the increasingly complex self-images that children develop as they continue through grade school and into their high school years. Throughout middle school and high school, young people are exposed to an ever-increasing variety of social contacts and learning experiences. These widening exposures to the world often result in a decrease in self-esteem as people acquire a more realistic understanding of their own abilities with maturity. A young boy, for example, may believe that he is a great ball thrower because throughout his childhood, his parents and grandparents have repeatedly told him how terrifically talented he is in that area. They have extravagantly praised every effort he has made. By the time he is ten, however, he has seen peers who are much better than he is at ball throwing. He has been subjected to peers bluntly telling him that his arm is not as strong as he thinks it is. Perhaps he is not even able to make the Little League team as a starter. The boy incorporates these experiences and social assessments into his self-image. His self-image is now more realistic than it was, and quite naturally, his self-esteem in the area of sports decreases. The boy is mature enough to think about what he has done, to reflect on the responses of others, and to begin to know himself for what he is and is not. This is not necessarily a bad thing, since a healthy self-image is not only positive but also accurate.

During adolescence, young people are increasingly capable of self-reflection, and as they interact with the environment, their major psychological job is to construct a self-image that is both positive and realistic. This is not an easy task. Teens have to deal with the changing physical aspects of their self-image as their bodies mature, as well as increasingly complex social challenges—academically, with peers, teachers, and other adults; and as part of becoming independent of their parents. They are often redefining themselves, learning to accept themselves, and figuring out where they fit into the larger world. Their definitions of self-image become less concrete and more abstract and complex as they develop ideas about their ethics, political and social standards, and general philosophies about life and society. Developing a stable identity and a realistic self-image has lifelong implications. Psychologist David Dean Witt explains, "Our identity is the single motivating force in life, in choosing behavior options, and in deciding on friends. Our self-image is all that stands between action and passivity, and it will continually change for most people over the remainder of their lives, depending on intelligence, experiences, and the quality of our social network."[7]

A Unique Identity and Meaningful Self-Image

The famous psychologist Erik Erikson theorized that all teens face a major identity crisis. They have to develop a unique sense of identity (self-image) that allows them to find the social environ-

What Matters Most?

All humans define their self-image in the three major categories of physical description, social roles, and personality traits. But how much emphasis is placed on which category seems to depend on culture. Some cultures, such American culture, emphasize independence and individuality. Other cultures, such as some Asian ones, emphasize the collective good, family, and group affiliation. These differences in cultural values affect how self-image is organized. When people are asked to give a series of statements describing themselves, Asians often tell their social roles first. They will describe, for example, being "Dan's good friend" or "the oldest daughter in the Lee family." They give more importance to social roles than Americans typically do. Americans are more likely to first describe traits that are individualistic and stress personality. They may say, for example, "I am a good student" or "I am resilient in the face of difficulties."

Of course, different ethnic groups within a larger society can have different cultures that affect self-image, too. In 2010 a group of researchers examined the "About Me" sections of people's Facebook pages to see which kinds of descriptions mattered most to different ethnic groups. In general, the researchers found that African Americans used descriptions that were the most independent and individualistic, Asian Americans used the most social role descriptions, and European Americans were somewhere in the middle.

ment where they belong and to form meaningful relationships with other people. They have to resolve any conflicts with their ideal image and their perceived self-image. And they have to achieve a sense of peace about who they are and their role in the world. Erikson writes, "In the social jungle of human existence, there is no feeling of being alive without a sense of identity."[8]

During their high school years, teens identify their strengths and weaknesses more or less accurately. For younger adolescents of about twelve or thirteen, however, the hardest aspect of self-image to adjust to is physical appearance because it is dramatically changing, and self-image has to conform to those changes. Teens are coping with changes such as growth spurts, increases

A young boy may believe he is an exceptional athlete as his parents continually encouraged him with false praise of his abilities. However, by ten years old he can recognize in comparison to his peers whether he is truly talented.

in hormone production, voice alterations, body shape differences, and acne. At the same time, they are highly aware of and sensitive to the idea that others are looking at and evaluating them. They reflect on these perceived evaluations and form new schemas of self-image based on their appearance. In one large study of teens in Germany, the researchers discovered that a positive self-image and healthy self-esteem were largely determined by how positively teens viewed their physical appearance. Appearance was more important for these teens than academic achievement, positive social skills and interactions, parental relationships, or teacher approval. The study's authors suggest, "As one's appearance is the first thing others perceive, this may explain the importance of one's self-perceived looks for overall self-esteem we identified here."[9] In other words, each individual teen is acutely aware that he or she initially judges people on appearance, so he or she assumes the same judgment comes from other people and bases positive or negative self-image on those perceptions. At this time, teens are evaluating themselves more on external standards than on their own internal evaluations of themselves and who they are.

As teens get older, however, according to professor of human development David H. Demo, they "become less susceptible to evaluations by others."[10] By about age sixteen, they are learning more about what kind of a person they truly are and what characteristics identify them as a whole and bring them satisfaction. They learn to be comfortable with their body and appearance, to choose positive social roles, and to internally evaluate their strengths, talents, and skills, perhaps accepting weaknesses as not all that important to them. For example, a young woman may know that she will never be a movie star but still be content with her appearance; she values her intelligence and enjoys her roles as friend, student, daughter, and dating partner, while looking forward to possible future roles in a career and as a wife or mother. Demo says that self-image stabilizes and solidifies during this adolescent period, and people feel better about themselves. He explains, "Self-cognitions [thoughts about self] are reorganized and reintegrated, self-consciousness wanes, stability of self is restored, and levels of self-esteem rise steadily as individuals move through this developmental period."[11]

WORDS IN CONTEXT

cognition

A mental process, such as thinking, knowing, remembering, and judging.

The Dynamic Self-Image

A mature self-image is established during adolescence, but that does not mean that self-image remains the same throughout a person's life. Demo says, "Self-concept is a structure but it is also a process. It is stable but it also changes."[12] As a process, self-image grows and changes throughout one's life, based on social interactions, experiences, and cognitive ability. During each individual's lifetime, that dynamic self-image determines what a person is able to do, what actions he or she decides to take, and how successfully the individual crafts a fulfilling and happy life. Each individual's feelings about his or her self-image determine self-esteem, self-confidence, and overall psychological health.

CHAPTER 2

Positive Self-Image and High Self-Esteem

Is an individual's self-image mostly positive or mostly negative? The answer to that question determines how that person feels about himself or herself in general. The more positive self-image is as a whole, the higher self-esteem is. People talk about the benefits of good self-esteem, but they often do not really know what that means. To social psychologists, self-esteem is a measure of how positively or negatively people feel about themselves, especially how closely this perception matches their view of their ideal selves. Self-esteem is not dependent on just one trait or aspect of a person, such as intelligence or popularity. It is an overall evaluation of the self that tends to remain stable over time. People see themselves, in general, either as good and worthy or inadequate and less worthy.

In part, however, even overall self-esteem can vary from day to day or from moment to moment, depending on experiences. That is because how people feel about themselves is often dependent on whether they believe others are viewing them positively. For instance, a young man who has just delivered a successful speech and received much applause and praise will bask in the accomplishment and feel his self-esteem rising. That same young man may feel his self-esteem fall after being dumped by his girlfriend. Nevertheless, a person's overall sense of worth and adequacy generally overcomes temporary failures and bad experiences as time passes. If he or she has developed an identity as a good and worthwhile person, then both self-image and ongoing self-evaluation remain positive.

Maturity and Self-Esteem

Most people maintain a positive self-image and relatively high self-esteem. Several factors determine a person's self-esteem. One important factor is age. Many studies have found that from middle adolescence and into adulthood, self-esteem rises steadily until people are in their late sixties. In some studies, people were followed over several years and retested for self-esteem periodically. In other studies, large numbers of people of all different ages were evaluated for their levels of self-esteem. No matter what the study method, the results held true—self-esteem increases with age. Psychologists call this phenomenon the "maturity principle." They theorize that during the teen years, it is normal for people to be confused about their self-identity and unsure about how they fit into society, what their roles are, and how well their actual selves match their ideal selves. As people mature, however, they find acceptable social roles, establish good social relationships, and feel both comfortable and confident with their place in the world.

Psychologist Charles Stangor believes that the rise in self-esteem with maturity is related to the comparisons between the ideal self and the actual self that everyone makes. He explains that when a person's perceived self-image is largely different from the person's ideal self, then self-esteem drops. The closer the ideal is to reality, the higher self-esteem is. Stangor asks, "Could it be that older adults have a current view of self that is closer to their ideal than younger adults, and that this is why their self-esteem is often higher?" Some evaluations of adults do provide evidence that elderly adults see their self-image and their ideal self as more alike than do younger adults. Stangor uses this evidence to conclude, "In part, older adults are able to more closely align these two selves because they are better able to realistically adjust their ideal standards as they age . . . and because they engage in more favorable and age-appropriate social comparisons than do younger

> **WORDS IN CONTEXT**
>
> **self-identity**
>
> The overall, generally permanent understanding a person has of himself or herself.

21

adults."[13] This seems to be true both for young adults and middle-aged adults. Compared to younger people, older adults less often try to be someone they are not. They are comfortable in their own skin. They have chosen social groups in which they are accepted and appreciated. They engage in activities in which they have determined that they can be successful. They are not experimenting with different behaviors and social roles to which they are not suited.

In a practical sense, mature adults also often have achieved a relatively high status in their career, which would increase their sense of self-worth. They are typically free of the burdens of child rearing and can concentrate on their work, relationships, social

Self-esteem can vary from day to day. A young man experiencing a rise in confidence from his successful speech at school may then lose self-esteem when his girlfriend breaks up with him the next day.

roles, and larger community. They can devote their energies to self-improvement and self-reflection. Perhaps these circumstances, too, contribute to positive self-image and high self-esteem.

Complexity and Self-Esteem

Self-esteem rises throughout a lifetime, but that does not mean that younger people cannot have a positive self-image and good self-esteem. One factor in maintaining that positive self-image, even in the face of bad experiences, is self-complexity. A complex self-image is one that is rich in different ways of thinking about the self. It includes a variety of social roles, past and present experiences, future goals, and varied personal traits. Stangor says:

> For example, imagine a woman whose self-concept contains the social identities of *student*, *girlfriend*, *daughter*, *psychology student*, and *tennis player* and who has encountered a wide variety of life experiences. Social psychologists would say that she has high self-complexity. On the other hand, a man who perceives himself primarily as either a student or as a member of the soccer team and who has had a relatively narrow range of life experiences would be said to have low self-complexity.[14]

The woman who is high in self-complexity may face a difficult event, such as failing a psychology class or suffering an injury that prevents her from playing tennis. Although either circumstance would be hard to accept, she could turn to other interests and roles where she still feels successful. She could maintain her overall positive self-image, and her self-esteem would remain intact. The man who is low in self-complexity, however, might suffer a devastating blow to his self-esteem if a serious injury permanently ended his soccer career. Soccer was one of the few roles that defined his

WORDS IN CONTEXT

self-complexity
A description of self-image that refers to how many various aspects and roles are a part of a person's self-knowledge.

positive self-image. His negative feelings about losing that identity when he has few other roles to take the place of soccer could lead to low self-esteem. Everyone has to deal with disappointments and failure, but in general, failures hurt less when they do not damage overall self-image. A person with self-complexity is usually happier and psychologically healthier because self-esteem is not threatened by one failure, however large it may seem to be at the time. Of course, a soccer player who never loses that role and remains a star athlete throughout his or her career will also maintain high self-esteem, no matter how lacking in complexity his or her self-image is. Complexity is just one factor that affects self-esteem.

The Benefits of High Self-Esteem

Psychologically, people with high self-esteem experience several benefits, no matter what their age or self-complexity. People with high self-esteem are confident about their own abilities. They are able to make choices, strive for goals, trust their own judgment, and overcome problems. They believe that they are able to accomplish their undertakings and experience success. In general, people with high self-esteem are therefore optimistic. Even in childhood, such individuals feel positive about themselves and the world and expect good things to happen to them. High self-esteem also allows people not to worry too much about what others think of them. They can engage in social interactions comfortably and without fear that others are looking at them and judging them poorly.

Those with high self-esteem also have achieved self-acceptance. This means that they accept themselves for who they are and do not wish to be someone else. They know they have faults and flaws, but overall they are happy with themselves. Finally, people with good self-esteem are resilient. Just as all people do, they deal with negative life events, but they are able to bounce back from life's blows and overcome them. The University of California–Davis Health Center sums up, "Self-esteem affects our trust in others, our relationships, our work—nearly every part of our lives. Positive self-esteem gives us the strength and

Self-Esteem in the Elderly

Even though self-esteem rises as people get older, it does begin to decrease again as people get into their seventies, eighties, and nineties. Approximately one-third of these elderly people have low self-esteem. Psychologists speculate that the decline in self-esteem in old age is related to developing significant physical health issues, losing significant social relationships through death, and perhaps losing a feeling of having a purpose in life. The other main issue identified with a lower self-esteem in elderly people is a decline in socioeconomic status. This means that the elderly are seen as having less value in society when they retire and often experience lower income than they had before they retired. Not every older person experiences lower self-esteem, but many are at risk. On average, those with poor health are most affected.

flexibility to take charge of our lives and grow from our mistakes without the fear of rejection."[15]

David Dean Witt says that positive self-esteem is actually "high social competence, which simply means the effective management of events involving others."[16] He describes some of the behaviors in social situations that are evident in people with high self-esteem. For instance, these people comfortably make eye contact when they are talking with others. They can cooperate with others in group activities, but they are also able to take on leadership roles and give directions when appropriate. They approach other people in a friendly way, initiate conversations, and are willing to express their own opinions. In short, people with high self-esteem are usually good with social relationships and make other people feel comfortable, too.

Developing High Self-Esteem

High self-esteem begins to develop in childhood from parents who are nurturing and supportive of the child's personality, temperament, and identity. Parents who are warm and loving and enjoy the company of their child teach the child that he or she is an

People who have high self-esteem generally function well in social situations. They comfortably make eye contact when talking with others.

enjoyable companion and worthy of love and attention. Parents who teach their children how to do things and encourage independent efforts are teaching their children that they are capable and to be proud of their accomplishments and abilities. Parents who appreciate their quiet, bookish child's temperament instead of wishing for an active, outgoing, energetic child demonstrate that the child's natural tendencies are not only OK but positive.

Children also need to be treated with respect if they are to develop high self-esteem. This means treating the child's feelings as legitimate and being sincerely interested in what the child has to say. It means recognizing that even a young child has a right to make some decisions and learn that his or her social communications are important. Psychologist Nathaniel Branden offers an example from his own personal experience:

> One day, I was swinging my granddaughter around by the arms. This was something she loved. But at some point, she said, "Let me down, Grandpa." But because I was having so much fun myself, I continued to swing her. She said, "Grandpa, you're not listening." And I immediately realized that I wasn't and set her back down on the floor. By listening to what my granddaughter said, I treated her feelings with respect. A child who is not allowed to have a voice in what happens to him will not feel entitled to his own views as an adult.[17]

Branden's granddaughter was learning that she could have her own views and developing good self-esteem.

The right kind of praise from parents also helps develop high self-esteem. Praise that helps develop self-esteem is both descriptive and specific. It describes what the child did, such as sticking with practicing the piano, instead of generalizing, such as "You're a great piano player" when the child is just a beginner. Descriptive praise allows the child to think about the good quality (persistence and effort) and feel competent and pleased with this part of his or her self-image. Saying someone is a great pianist, on the other hand, when he or she is able to play only simple tunes, can be understood as untrue, even by a young child.

Always hearing praise like "You are wonderful" is actually not very helpful for the development of self-esteem. Children know that such overpraising has not been earned. Good self-esteem comes from praise that is realistic as well as specific. For example, a boy who has played poorly at his soccer game does not need to be told he is a great player anyway. Praise that raises his self-esteem would be true, specific, and descriptive. The website KidsHealth suggests praise like, "I know that wasn't your best performance, but we all have off days. I'm proud of you for not giving up."[18] This kind of praise builds the positive self-image that leads to high self-esteem.

Maintaining High Self-Esteem

Of course, as children grow up, self-esteem continues to be affected by all social experiences. People respond to the reactions of others, compare themselves to their social groups, evaluate their careers and occupations, judge their social roles and relationships, and generally actively work to maintain and enhance self-esteem. A major way that people maintain high self-esteem is by actively seeking success in their experiences and their social roles. Many psychologists believe that much behavior is motivated by the need to feel a sense of self-worth and self-respect. This means searching for the things one is good at and continuing to do those things while avoiding those things that seem unlikely to bring success. People create positive lives for themselves and thus have high overall self-esteem. Stangor explains:

> One reason that many of us have positive self-esteem is because we are generally successful at creating positive lives. When we fail in one domain, we tend to move on until we find something that we are good at. We don't always expect to get the best grade on every test or to be the best player on the team. Therefore, we are often not surprised or hurt when those things don't happen. In short, we feel good about ourselves because we do a pretty good job at creating decent lives.[19]

Another way that people maintain and enhance self-esteem is by forming good relationships. In warm, congenial friendships and loving relationships, people find others who approve of and appreciate them. This makes people feel good about themselves and increases the feeling of self-worth. A sense of belonging in a social group is a powerful way to raise self-esteem.

In modern times the connections people have on social media sites often contribute to positive feelings of self-esteem. In 2014 Stephanie Tobin and her research team from the Univer-

Many psychologists believe that behavior is motivated by a desire to feel a sense of self-worth and accomplishment. This means searching for things one is good at and avoiding things that are unlikely to bring success.

sity of Queensland in Australia studied the effects of Facebook on people's sense of belonging and self-worth. The researchers asked a group of regular Facebook users to post and comment on temporary Facebook pages set up by the researchers. Every participant was told that all the others in the study group could see and comment on their posts. With half the group, however, the researchers arranged the situation so that no one could see,

A Quick Test of Self-Esteem

The Alamo Mental Health Group of San Antonio, Texas, says that if you can agree with at least five of the following statements, you have good self-esteem.

- I do not feel I must always please other people.
- I generally feel that I like myself.
- I speak up for myself and feel I have rights.
- I am happy most of the time.
- I feel that my struggles are normal ones and not my fault.
- I do not need to prove that I am better than others.
- I do not need constant validation or approval from others.
- I can make friends easily.
- I feel good about myself without praise from others.
- I feel pleased, rather than envious, when those I care about have success in life.

Lee Scheingold, "Self-Esteem," Alamo Mental Health Group. http://alamomentalhealth.com.

like, or comment on their posts. Then the researchers interviewed each participant about their feelings of self-esteem, self-respect, and how meaningful they thought their lives were in general. The study participants who received no feedback on their posts all showed lower self-esteem and described themselves as of less importance in the world than did the half whose posts were responded to and liked by other users. Tobin and her team describe this study as one piece of evidence that Facebook participation gives users a feeling of belonging and positive self-esteem. That result partially explains why social media is so popular.

High self-esteem is so important that most people often enhance it by distorting reality. For instance, people pat themselves on the back, so to speak, for successes in their lives but blame failures on others. They remember past behaviors and events as more positive than they actually were. Commonly, they think of themselves as more honest than other people or as better vehicle drivers or as more popular than they really are. Stangor says, "We emphasize our positive characteristics, and we may even in some cases distort information—all to help us maintain positive self-esteem."[20]

Can Self-Esteem Be Too High?

For the most part, efforts to view the self positively are natural and harmless. They help people feel optimistic and successful in their lives. Sometimes, however, people can have too much self-esteem. They can so exaggerate their self-worth and distort reality that other people reject them. An unrealistic and overly high self-esteem can hurt an individual and his or her relationships with others. Narcissism is a psychological trait in which people have an exaggerated sense of their own importance and overly high self-esteem. Such people are also self-centered and lack empathy for others. A narcissist's self-image and self-esteem are not based on the evaluations and judgments of others or on an accurate interpretation of events and experiences. Instead, the narcissist's self-image is a false self-image, and other people interpret the self-esteem as undeserved. A narcissistic person often has poor relationships, is a bully, and is selfish. Extremely high self-esteem does not lead to positive outcomes in life. It is of little value if it is used to ignore the needs of others and to deny any negative aspects of the self that all people have.

> **WORDS IN CONTEXT**
>
> **narcissism**
>
> A psychological disorder characterized by exaggerated self-esteem, a need to be constantly admired, and a disregard for others' feelings.

Everyone wants to have high self-esteem, but it has to be balanced with thoughtfulness and a desire for truth. Stangor says, "As in many other domains, then, having positive self-esteem is a good thing, but we must be careful to temper it with a healthy realism and a concern for others."[21] Sometimes, the people with the best, most loving relationships and the most success are those who are not always satisfied with who they are.

CHAPTER 3

Negative Self-Image and Low Self-Esteem

Most people in the West, when assessed psychologically, have an adequate amount of self-esteem and a generally positive overall self-image. Some people, however, have a persistent feeling of inadequacy and worthlessness and suffer from very low self-esteem. This situation can be normal for adolescents as they struggle to establish a self-identity and find their place in the social structure of their environment. Teens may often feel overly self-conscious and worried about the judgments of others. They may be extremely critical of themselves as they compare their own self-images to their ideal selves. Usually, teens work through these feelings successfully. For those who cannot, whether as teens or adults, low self-esteem can be crippling and lead to long-lasting low self-confidence, depression, and anxiety.

What It Feels Like

No matter their age, people with very low self-esteem have several characteristics in common. Low self-esteem often means low self-confidence. Especially in social situations, people with low self-esteem are shy, withdrawn, and unable to express themselves effectively. They usually feel awkward and worry that they stand out in a negative way. Self-consciousness is high; people feel that others are looking at them and judging them, even when no one is really paying them any attention. They can interpret other people's comments as critical, even when no criticism is intended.

Instead of trying to get ahead or learn new things, people with low self-esteem concentrate on not making mistakes. They are very afraid of failure and try hard to avoid it. They are pessimistic rather than optimistic, expecting experiences to turn out badly, to be disliked, or to make mistakes. Low self-esteem leads to low self-respect and a low sense of self-worth, all stemming from a poor self-image that is based on false beliefs about the self. Some of these false beliefs are that the individual's opinions do not matter much, that he or she does not deserve to be respected by others, and that his or her feelings are somehow wrong or illegitimate. Deep down, people with low self-esteem believe that they are unlovable and unlikable. Their self-image is full of negative schemas.

Children with low self-esteem are often underachieving and undermotivated in school. They do not want to try to do their work and give up easily when asked to learn a new task. Teachers often describe such children either as unhappy and insecure or as acting out in angry, hostile ways. Some children may avoid social interactions and schoolwork, acting shy and withdrawn in social situations and easily quitting when things get too hard. These children may be easily bullied by others. Other children with low self-esteem, however, may become bullies as they try to make themselves feel more important. They may cheat on schoolwork, mainly because of a fear of failure or looking bad in the eyes of others.

As adults, people with very low self-esteem often experience distress and unhappiness about themselves and their social roles. They continue to have inaccurate ideas about themselves and to feel unworthy and inadequate. Even if they do not think they are terrible people, they view themselves as mediocre and feel uncertain about themselves. They remain pessimistic. Instead of trying to enhance self-esteem, they spend their psychological energy just trying to protect themselves from failure, whether in relationships or in life experiences. People with low self-esteem want to be likable, lovable, and successful, but they doubt that they can achieve the positive outcomes they seek. They have low self-confidence.

People with low confidence tend to be shy and withdrawn. They sometimes think others are judging them even when no one is paying them any attention.

The Disadvantages of Low Self-Esteem

Psychologists have discovered that people with low self-esteem are more emotionally vulnerable than those with adequate self-esteem. They are more likely to have emotional highs and lows and to be more strongly affected by negative experiences. Psychologists Roy F. Baumeister and Brad Bushman say that "misfortune hits them harder." They explain, "If at first they don't succeed, people with high self-esteem are willing to try again harder, whereas people with low self-esteem are more likely to give up. Most broadly, people with high self-esteem are happier than people with low self-esteem."[22]

Unhappiness is the major disadvantage of low self-esteem. People with high self-esteem are not smarter than those with low self-esteem. They do not get better grades in school because of positive self-esteem. They are not better looking or more popular. They are not more successful in life, nor do they better avoid damaging behaviors such as drug addiction or violent actions. Over and over again, psychologists have tested the theories that self-esteem is responsible for good outcomes in life, but they have not found the theories to be true. Self-esteem seems to affect only how people feel. People with low self-esteem lack confidence in themselves and feel unhappy about themselves and their lives.

Low self-esteem also seems to increase the risk of anxiety and depression. People with very low self-esteem who avoid experiences out of a fear of failure or hide away from interacting with other people may be damaging their mental health. Psychiatrist Chris Williams explains, "In the short term, avoiding challenging and difficult situations makes you feel a lot safer. In the longer term, this can

backfire because it reinforces your underlying doubts and fears. It teaches you the unhelpful rule that the only way to cope is by avoiding things."[23] Over time, reinforcing doubts and fears can lead to persistent sadness, feelings of helplessness, constant worrying, panic when out of one's safe space, loneliness, inability to cope with day-to-day situations, and an overall belief that nothing can ever get better. These are the hallmarks of depression and anxiety disorders.

What Causes Low Self-Esteem?

Low self-esteem can be a lifelong problem, but it usually begins in childhood with the development of a poor self-image. Low self-esteem is learned. Parenting styles can be a major cause of low self-esteem. For example, overly critical parents may teach their children to believe that they are not worthwhile. Critical parents might say to a child, perhaps a young boy, "You are always so lazy." They might complain, "Why are you so dumb?" "Haven't you got any sense?" "You never listen!" "You have two left feet; you are so awkward, you are always stumbling over things!" Even if he resents and gets angry about such statements, the boy incorporates them into his beliefs about himself. The criticisms

Teens and Low Self-Esteem

Kristine Tye is a marriage and family therapist who specializes in working with teens. She describes three causes of low self-esteem in teens that can be troublesome. First, she says, teens can have difficulty handling emotions. She explains, "Teens have difficulty identifying feelings, responding to feelings, and remembering that feelings are not permanent. Adults struggle with this, too; however, for a teen, these experiences of emotional turmoil are much more intense." She encourages teens to be kind to themselves, to resist being afraid of their negative emotions, and to learn to explore and accept their feelings. The second cause is being stuck in negative thought patterns. This means constantly worrying about things or expecting bad things to happen. Negative thinking can become a habit that causes low self-esteem. Tye suggests that fears and worries have to be faced but also that teens need to practice noticing the positive things that happen in life. The third cause of low self-esteem in teens is in the area of communication. Teens often lack positive communications with parents or other supportive adults because they are becoming independent and not talking with adults as much as they did as children. At the same time, they may receive negative communications from peers in the form of bullying or criticisms. Tye believes that teens need to find and relate to supportive adults who can help with self-esteem.

Kristine Tye, "3 Causes of Low Self-Esteem in Teens (and What to Do About It)," Stop Medicine Abuse, April 21, 2016. http://stopmedicineabuse.org.

become supposed facts about himself that he weaves into his developing self-image. These ideas lead to a poor self-image and thus low self-esteem, as he accepts that he is awkward, lazy, or stupid in comparison to other people.

Parents can also communicate criticisms nonverbally. As an example, psychologist and therapist Ronald Mah describes one critical mother talking to her son about his schoolwork:

> "You can do that. You are smart enough to do that. I don't understand why you aren't doing better." And as she said that, she shook her head and frowned, her eyes rolled up

in her head and she let out a deep sigh. . . . While her verbal communication seems to say that she thinks her son is smart, her nonverbal communications are also very clear. Her nonverbal communications are saying that he is letting her down (she is disappointed in him), and there the must be something wrong with him. This is the inadvertent communication that destroys Self-Esteem. . . . The verbal communication was positive, however, her nonverbal communication—the shake of her head, the frown, the eyes rolling and the deep sigh was very negative. The son believed the nonverbal communication, and Self-Esteem is harmed . . . again).[24]

Similarly, teachers and other important adults in a child's life can harm his or her self-esteem with harsh criticism. This does not mean that adults cannot instruct children or act as authority figures or even point out failures. But it does mean that communications that attack a child's sense of self and of self-worth rather than being specific and descriptive about how to change are harmful. Children who experience too much shame, guilt, or feelings of worthlessness as a result of adult criticism are likely to develop low self-esteem.

Severe criticism is not the only way that adults can cause a poor self-image in children. Not surprisingly, parents who are abusive or extremely neglectful and uncaring can cause low self-esteem in their children, but sometimes parents who are overly involved in their children's lives can cause low self-esteem, too. Narcissistic parents, for instance, try to live through their children. They give the impression that the child is worthy only if the child is meeting the parents' needs, whether impressing other people, always being there for the parent, or simply never having any independence or needs of one's own. Everyone wants to be proud of

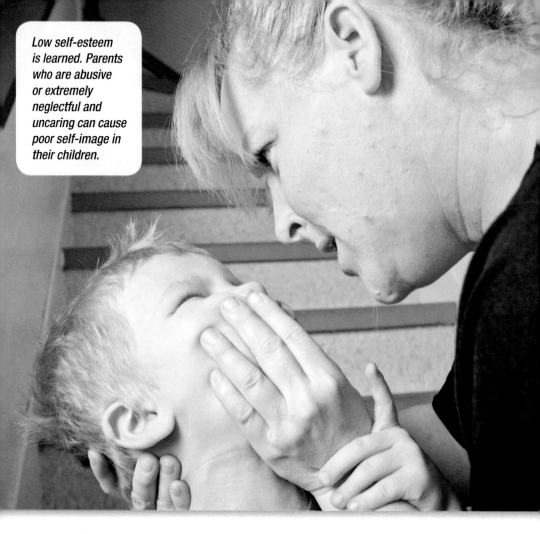

their children, but narcissistic parents are excessively involved in feeling good through their children. Preston Ni, professor of communication studies at Foothill College in Silicon Valley, California, gives some examples of how narcissistic parents use their children instead of loving those children for who they are. One father he quotes says, "If my son doesn't grow up to be a professional baseball player, I'll shoot 'em!" A woman describes her mother's behavior by saying, "My mom used to love dolling me up in cute dresses, even though I was a tomboy by nature. I think she felt that when I received compliments for my appearance, she looked good in reflection. It boosted her self-worth."[25] People who grow up with narcissistic parents often feel as if their thoughts and feelings are of little worth. They can believe that they are never good enough.

Disability and Self-Esteem

Difficult parents are not the only factors that can lead to low self-esteem. Social problems in school, in the larger community, and in personal interactions can sometimes be to blame. People with attention-deficit/hyperactivity disorder (ADHD), for instance, often compare themselves to other people and feel inadequate. As children, people with ADHD are commonly criticized for their behaviors by parents and teachers. These children cannot control their activity levels, their inattention, or their academic struggles, yet they are very aware that other children can. Since they do not fit in, other children may tease, bully, or reject them. Psychotherapist Terry Matlen explains, "If they've grown up hearing over and over again that they are 'bad, incapable or even stupid,' these words hang on to them and they begin to define themselves as such."[26] That is the very definition of a poor self-image and low self-esteem. It can affect any child with any disability who feels too different and not normal.

Even as adults, people with ADHD often continue to suffer from low self-esteem. At work, they can continue to have trouble concentrating and completing tasks. They may still have trouble controlling impulses or emotional reactions to other people. Although most adults with ADHD successfully adapt to their difficulties, their self-esteem may continue to be an issue. Their self-image is based on other people's apparent opinions of them throughout their years, and the person with ADHD may be constantly critical of himself or herself as a result. This internal criticism means low self-esteem. No matter how successful in a career or in relationships, a person with ADHD may still feel stupid, awkward, bad, or just different. Dr. Gabor Mate describes one woman who feels she is not as capable as other people, even though she has a college degree and is obviously intelligent. She told Mate, "I feel so dumb. I can never keep up with discussions. People talk about politics and current affairs, and I have no head for those things. I try to remember facts and names from the newspaper, but they don't stick. I tune out when people talk to me."[27] This woman is doing well in life but still is unhappy with her self-image and thinks about her perceived negative traits while forgetting about the positive ones.

Any disability can make it hard for a person to develop a positive self-image and high self-esteem. Psychological counselor Ryan J. Voigt at the University of Wisconsin–Eau Claire explains:

> One added challenge for a person with a disability may be viewing him or herself as a person first. A disability is only one facet of a person. . . . Another issue for people with disabilities may be dealing with discrimination and stereotypes from society. Our society places emphasis on looks, speed, and being the same as everyone else. Thus, people with disabilities might place additional pressure on themselves to try to meet society's impossible standards.[28]

A person with a disability faces two challenges to self-esteem. He or she must struggle with his or her internal self-image that treats the disability as the most important schema and also with the way other people actually respond and react, often dismissively or with prejudice. In instances like this, it is the larger community and the culture that can be a major cause of low self-esteem.

Learned from One's Culture

The culture one grows up in can affect self-esteem for everyone, not only those with disabilities. In Western cultures, in which individualism and individual freedoms and rights are highly valued, having high self-esteem is usually considered very important. That means people strive to develop good self-esteem, and most succeed in achieving it. In collectivist Eastern cultures, where the group and the community are more highly valued, self-esteem generally is not as emphasized. In repeated studies, psychological researchers have found that people from these Eastern cultures have lower self-esteem overall than people in Western cultures. These studies demonstrate how much self-image and self-esteem are determined by learning and how social roles and expectations affect self-esteem.

In one study, the researchers found evidence that the lower self-esteem in collectivist cultures was related to the trait of mod-

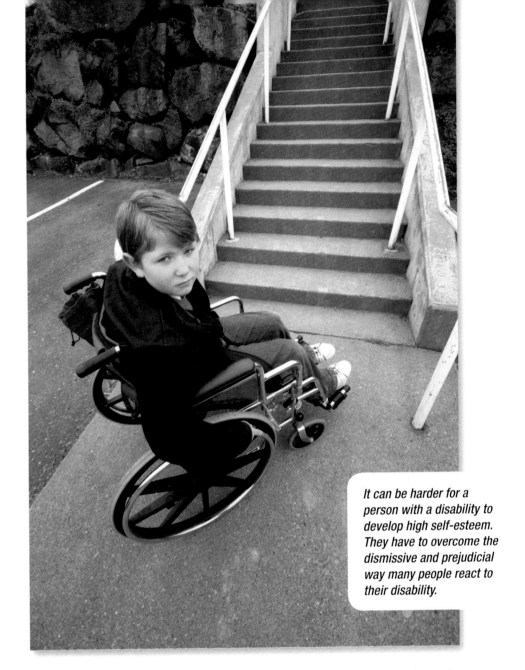

It can be harder for a person with a disability to develop high self-esteem. They have to overcome the dismissive and prejudicial way many people react to their disability.

esty. People in these cultures value modesty much more than do people in individualistic cultures. They do not work to enhance self-esteem as people in the Western world seem to do. Yet cultures that emphasize modesty do not produce more unhappy people than Western cultures. Lower self-esteem is not necessarily bad for psychological health if people live in a culture that does not stress the importance of good self-esteem.

Success, Fame, and Self-Esteem

No matter how successful people become in life, they do not necessarily escape low self-esteem. Many tremendously talented people have grappled with not being satisfied with who they are. Superstar singer Mariah Carey, for example, admits, "I've always had really low self-esteem, and I still do." Actress Kate Winslet grew up battling overweight and a poor self-image. Classmates teased her and nicknamed her "Blubber." Today she still fights to remain positive about herself. She says, "Even now I do not consider myself to be some kind of great, sexy beauty. Absolutely not." Tennis champion Serena Williams has dealt with self-esteem issues as well. Growing up, she wanted to be like her older sister, Venus, instead of being herself. She says she always tried to copy her sister and had a hard time believing in herself as good enough. She explains, "It was tough for me to stop being Venus and become the person I am." Finding self-acceptance and feeling worthwhile can be difficult for all sorts of people.

Quoted in Anneli Rufus, "5 Superstars Who Have Talked About Their Low Self-Esteem," *HuffPost* (blog), February 12, 2014. www.huffingtonpost.com.

Gender and Self-Esteem

Traditionally, one other important factor makes a difference in levels of self-esteem. That factor is gender. On average, women have lower self-esteem than men and have for decades—ever since psychologists have been studying self-esteem. In 2016 the American Psychological Association reported on the publication of a large study that measured the self-esteem of 985,000 adult men and women in forty-eight different countries. In every country, even in developed Western ones where gender equality is greater, women reported lower self-esteem than men. The result held true in every culture that the researchers studied. Lead researcher Wiebke Bleidorn says, "We were really surprised by the remarkable degree of similarity across cultures."[29]

The researchers are not sure why women around the world have lower self-esteem, but they have speculated about the cause. Perhaps, says Bleidorn, it is caused at least in part by inborn biological differences. Almost every psychological trait has some genetic basis, and Bleidorn thinks it possible that self-esteem and confidence in one's own skills do, too. Perhaps also the traditional gender roles that have existed throughout human history play a part. Women and men have always divided responsibilities by gender, such as with cooking, child rearing, hunting, and careers. Maybe, says Bleidorn, this history still affects women, even in the most progressive societies. The researchers suggest that the result of this study provides evidence that self-esteem is partially based on how important the culture views each person's role in life. Women have seen their roles viewed as less important than men's and thus have lower self-esteem.

Gender differences in self-esteem do not mean that women cannot be as successful as men. Many psychologists believe that women's self-esteem will be more equal to men's as their positions in society improve, as the gender gap in salary closes, and as women generally assume more powerful social roles. However, even the most successful women today still may face more self-doubt and worries about inadequacy than men do. The good news is that throughout their lifetime, women and men, people with disabilities, and those who grew up under difficult circumstances can all change their self-image and self-esteem. People can make new choices, stop depending on the evaluations of others, and gather more accurate information about themselves. No one is stuck with low self-esteem for life.

CHAPTER 4

What About Body Image?

Body image refers to how a person thinks, feels, and reacts to his or her physical attributes. A person with a healthy body image feels attractive and acceptable and is comfortable in his or her own skin. An unhealthy body image means the person is unhappy and dissatisfied with how he or she looks and wants to drastically change that appearance. Body image does not necessarily describe a person's physical appearance accurately. Instead, it is the way the person perceives his or her attributes that matters. Body image is about physical appearance, but it is also about an individual's attitude, feelings, and beliefs about that image. It is about comparing one's body to the standards a person learns from his or her society and culture. Just as with a person's beliefs about personality traits and characteristics, body image is strongly connected to an individual's self-image and self-esteem.

Body image can be positive, negative, or somewhere in between. It can include obvious attributes such as being tall or short, having brown or blue eyes, having curly or straight hair, or being slender or overweight. It can also include subjective evaluations, such as being pretty or powerfully brawny. It can mean judging that one's nose is unsightly or one's feet are too big or being satisfied or dissatisfied with one's body shape. Body image is what each person sees in the mirror, but that perception is not what the eyes see; it is what the mind thinks it sees in the looking glass reflection.

Children and Body Image

Each person's body image begins to develop in childhood, but bodies change, and body image continually changes as people grow older. It is influenced by many factors, including family, friends, peers, media, and culture. In early childhood, at three or four years old, body image seems to emphasize size and weight. Most little children have fairly healthy body images. They are generally satisfied with how they believe they look and do not express unhappiness with their physical traits. But small children already have ideas about what bodies should look like. Australian psychologist Susan Paxton is conducting long-term body image studies of children and has been collecting data since 2011. Paxton says that the children have already developed "weight biases"; one of her findings so far is that four-year-olds already believe that thin bodies are better than heavier ones.

WORDS IN CONTEXT

subjective

Based on or influenced by one's own feelings and opinions.

Nevertheless, these young children tend to see themselves as quite thin and of a small size. As a matter of fact, they often express the desire to be bigger in size. Paxton says, "We think that four-year-old children associated being a bit bigger with growing up, and boys especially appear to want to be a bit bigger than they are."[30]

Paxton and her research team do not yet know for sure what influences are most important in determining children's beliefs about body image and what ideal bodies look like. They are exploring the idea that peers and media such as television and movies are important factors. Paxton explains, "We think we are seeing body size stereotypes developing early in children as they are reflected in the world around them, and these attitudes reflect the societal importance of thinness for females and leanness and muscularity for males. These ideals are typically unachievable but are reflected in so many different ways, including media, but even children's storybooks and cartoons."[31]

Studies have shown that many four-year-olds, particularly boys, wish they were bigger in size. They associate being physically larger with growing up.

Fashion Dolls and Superheroes

Unachievable and unrealistic body types continue to influence children's views of their own bodies as they get older. Barbie dolls, for instance, are a part of the culture for American girls. According to the American Psychiatric Association, 99 percent of girls in the United States own at least one Barbie doll. Many psychologists believe that the doll's body shape and looks become the ideal body type to little girls who play with them. Although the manufacturer now produces Barbie dolls that look more like average women, many girls still have the traditional Barbie—whose shape is impossible for a real girl or woman to achieve. Psychologists say that the unrealistic standards can lead many children to become unhappy with their own bodies. In one 2016 study, for example, little girls six to eight years old who played with traditional Barbie dolls in a research setting later expressed more insecurity about their own bodies and more dissatisfaction with themselves than girls who played with realistic dolls. These girls are growing up in a society that values thinness and a perfect shape and are absorbing the messages about what makes for a positive body image. Naturally, those messages affect their own body images, even at this young age.

Little boys can be affected by society's messages about perfect bodies, too. Action figures, for instance, often have exaggerated physical proportions and huge muscles. Many experts are concerned that playing with these toys affects the body images of boys and teaches them unrealistic standards just as Barbie dolls do with girls. Timothy Baghurst, a professor of physical education, says that boys can develop anxiety about their own bodies that lasts even into adulthood. He explains, "I don't mean to say that we shouldn't encourage a healthy physique in the toys we create for boys, but healthy is the key term. As they are, many toy figures for boys are unhealthily proportioned and could serve as a catalyst for unhealthy mental and physical behaviours."[32] In other words, boys can develop a poor body image as they grow up and keep trying for a body shape that is impossible to achieve.

It is not only toys that affect children's body images. Parents who talk about being unhappy with the imperfections of their own bodies may unintentionally influence their children to think about and worry about their bodies. Peers tease each other about body flaws, especially weight. Media representations of all sorts of people stress the importance of thinness or beauty or the right kind of clothing. In 2015 the nonprofit organization Common Sense Media released a report showing that children as young as five years old worry about what their bodies look like and think they should be thinner than they are. Between the ages of six and eight, more than half of all girls and one-third of boys think that they should be thinner than they are. Already, these children suffer from negative body image.

Teens and Body Image

If young children have trouble developing a healthy body image, it is even more difficult for teens. During adolescence, both boys and girls spend a lot of time thinking about their physical appearance and how they look. They can feel a lot of pressure to look, dress, and behave in a certain way. They are exposed to films, television shows, fashion and fitness magazines, advertising, and music that celebrate young, beautiful people with idealized, highly sexualized bodies. As a result, many teens are dissatisfied with their body image. In 2014 the *Today Show* and AOL did a survey of teen girls and discovered that 80 percent of them reported comparing their bodies to celebrities' bodies. Half of those girls also felt dissatisfied with their looks based on the comparisons.

Media and advertising consistently stress the importance of thinness and beauty. Peers will tease each other about body flaws, particularly weight. This will often lower one's self-esteem.

Body image has a direct, significant effect on self-esteem. Teens face at least three major issues in the development of positive self-esteem: academic competence, social relationships, and physical appearance. In 2016 a German psychological research team examined 2,950 students in secondary schools across Germany to determine which issue was most important for self-esteem. Students were of both genders, varied in age from ten to nineteen, and came from diverse backgrounds. The researchers reported, "Across all subgroups of a highly diverse secondary school sample, we found that students' self-esteem consistently hinges on how attractive they perceive themselves [to be]."[33] Social relationships and academic performance played a much smaller role in overall self-esteem. In addition, students who did not perceive themselves as attractive were much more likely to report being unhappy than those who did poorly in school or whose relationships were unsatisfactory. Girls' self-esteem was more affected by perceived good looks than boys', but boys, too, suffered when they felt unattractive.

Since a positive body image is so vital for self-esteem and a good overall feeling about oneself, a realistic evaluation of one's physical appearance is critical. Most teens do eventually work through their negative feelings about themselves, learn to accept their flaws and imperfections, and feel comfortable about their appearance. But some continue to struggle with body image into adulthood. Many adults have body image issues, too.

Why Body Image Matters

A healthy body image contributes to psychological health. It means liking and appreciating one's body and feeling comfortable and confident within it. People with a healthy body image are self-confident in social situations and are not overly worried that they are being judged by their looks. They know that their bodies are not perfect. They may think they have too many freckles or an unsightly mole or a nose that seems too large. But they do not feel that these flaws define their bodies. They realistically see all their unique good points, too. A positive body image helps people be physically healthy, leading them to actions such as eating nutritious food, dressing well in clean clothing, and exercising in a beneficial way. These people respect and care for their bodies.

An unhealthy body image leaves people feeling uncomfortable and awkward in their bodies. It is also almost always unrealistic and distorted. Flaws are emphasized, and parts of the body are disliked and seen as much worse than they are. People can become preoccupied with the negative aspects of their body and feel desperate to change them. They can believe that only other people are attractive while they themselves are shamefully unattractive and physical failures. Having an unhealthy body image can damage a person's social relationships and affect his or her overall happiness and self-acceptance. A negative body image is strongly associated with a negative self-image, low self-confidence, and poor self-esteem.

Starving to Be Perfect

One of the most dangerous consequences of a negative body image is an increased risk of eating disorders. Usually, eating disorders are related to an unhealthy obsession with weight and a negative body image in which the body is perceived as too fat. Anorexia nervosa, for example, is an eating disorder characterized by an intense desire to lose weight. People with anorexia starve themselves in pursuit of perfect thinness. Another major eating disorder is bulimia, a psychological condition in which a person binge eats and then forces vomiting or purging to avoid gaining weight. Both anorexia and bulimia are physically harmful and dangerous, as well as psychologically damaging. With both disorders, whether the person is of normal weight or emaciated, he or she looks in a mirror and truly perceives that he or she is overweight.

> ## WORDS IN CONTEXT
>
> **anorexia nervosa**
>
> An eating disorder in which there is an obsessive desire to lose weight and a refusal to eat.

Body Dysmorphic Disorder

Body dysmorphic disorder (BDD) is a severe psychological disorder in which body image is so distorted that the individual feels ugly, repulsive, and monstrous. It involves excessive and obsessive concern with a body part that the person thinks is terribly deformed, when in reality, other people do not even notice the supposed flaw. For example, an individual may think his ears stick out so much that they are disgusting or that her nose is so crooked that she cannot bear to be seen in public. People with BDD can spend hours a day staring in the mirror at their supposed deformity. They can feel so hideous that they are unable to allow other people to see them and thus cannot hold a job or even leave home. About one out of every two hundred people suffer with BDD, and it is extremely difficult to convince these people that there is nothing the matter with their body. They have extremely low self-esteem and feel worthless and completely unlovable. BDD is commonly treated with a combination of medication and cognitive behavioral therapy to help the patient learn to evaluate his or her body realistically.

Many people think that only girls and women develop eating disorders because of Western society's emphasis on female thinness and beauty, but psychiatrist Thomas Holbrook knows that is not true. Many males become obsessed with body image, too, and Holbrook was one of them. Even though he specialized in treating anorexic patients, for years he could not heal himself. His story is a good example of the disordered thinking that leads to distorted perceptions. After a knee injury that prevented him from running for exercise, Holbrook became terrified of getting fat and out of shape. He began to diet excessively. He found more exercises to do and obsessively spent hours a day on these workouts. His body image became so distorted that he could not see reality. He says, "Despite my efforts, my worst nightmare was happening. I felt and saw myself as fatter than ever before, even though I had started to lose weight. . . . I relied equally on my walking (up to six hours a day) and restrictive eating to fight fat, but it seemed I could never walk far enough or eat little enough."[34]

Holbrook's eating disorder spiraled out of control, and he grew emaciated and ill. He developed symptoms of malnutrition. But, he says, "even when I started feeling weak and tired, I did not understand."[35] He was trying to be physically fit, strong, and lean, but his body was shutting down. Finally, after years of abusing his body, Holbrook recognized that he was anorexic and began the process of recovery. He worked hard to make himself stop the compulsive exercising and eat normally. He also worked on understanding the emotions, distorted self-image, and negative body image that drove him into anorexia. He explains:

One of the most significant insights I've gained in my recovery has been that I have spent my whole life trying to be somebody I'm not. Just like so many of my patients, I had the feeling that I was never good enough. In my own estimation, I was a failure. Any compliments or recognition of achievement did not fit. On the contrary, I always expected to be "found out"—that others would discover that I was stupid, and it would be all over. Always starting with the premise that who I am is not good enough, I have gone to such extremes to improve what I assumed needed improvement. My eating disorder was one of those extremes.[36]

When males develop eating disorders, they often want to lose weight and gain more muscle mass. When females have eating disorders, they seem to concentrate simply on being thinner. More females than males develop eating disorders, but in

Negative body image can lead to dangerous eating disorders such as anorexia nervosa. Those with anorexia have an intense need to lose weight.

Western societies, where perfect bodies are celebrated in the media, both genders are vulnerable to the problem. And eating disorders tend to start in adolescence. Courtney, for example, was only thirteen when she became unhappy because she was overweight. She experimented with dieting and with making herself vomit when she thought she had eaten too much. Within a

When the Worst Really Happens

In the case of a sudden, scarring injury or a serious disease such as cancer, bodies really can change, and body image becomes an understandable problem. Young burn victims, for example, can look at their obvious, sometimes deforming scars and lose the positive body image they used to have. This can lead to increased risk of depression and low self-esteem. Recovering a positive body image and accepting the new normal can be a difficult issue. For teens and young adults, the biggest factor affecting their ability to feel good about themselves again is the support and reassurance they get from friends. Maintaining their self-esteem depends in large part on these positive social relationships.

For people with cancer, the changes in physical appearance usually involve necessary treatments. The side effects include hair loss, rashes, weight loss or gain, and surgical scars. Sometimes, the cancer patient loses a limb or an organ to the disease. Many of these issues resolve with time (for example, hair grows back when treatment is completed), but some, such as an amputation, are permanent. Adjusting to the changes and learning to accept and love one's body again can take a long time and a lot of work. The people who do best have supportive family and friends, connect with other people who have had cancer and understand the problems, and seek psychological counseling to help themselves work through their negative feelings.

year, her obsession with weight loss worsened. She remembers, "I had a journal where if I got really hungry I would sit there and write over and over about how I was not hungry. I drank diet Pepsi to fool my empty stomach. Soon I started to exercise too. I would run/walk on my treadmill and was doing 1000 jumping jacks a day. All of this seemed perfectly normal to me."[37] Courtney did lose a large amount of weight, but she developed physical problems. Throughout high school, she tried at times to eat better and stop vomiting, but she could not. Sometimes, she would make herself eat regular meals. "But then," she says, "I started to get scared that I was going to gain weight and get fat again so I started to throw up again."[38] This pattern continued until the young woman entered college and finally sought the psychological help she needed to improve her body image and raise her self-esteem.

Not Perfect but Still Just Fine

Eating disorders are an extreme manifestation of body dissatisfaction, but many people without an eating disorder struggle with the desire to meet society's standards of perfection. Psychological experts recommend that people recognize how impossible and unachievable cultural representations of perfect bodies really are. The images that people see in magazines, on the Internet, in films, and on television are airbrushed, filtered, and specially lit to make models and actors look better than they actually do. The majority of models today are 13 percent to 19 percent below a healthy weight. Ads for weight-loss products seem to try to make people disgusted with the body they have. A task force of the American Psychological Association concludes that these cultural standards damage self-image in young people and interfere with healthy development, which requires that people understand that there are different body types and no one can be perfect.

Actor Jennifer Lawrence believes that society is doing harm by emphasizing perfection. She wants to be a role model for a healthy body image, so she refuses to lose weight for Hollywood roles and wants to look "strong and healthy" instead of thin. She says about worrying over weight and size, "You have to look past it—you look how you look, and be comfortable. What are you going to do? Be hungry every single day to make other people happy? That's just dumb."[39] Experts agree that people need to learn to respect and accept their bodies and to celebrate their strengths instead of concentrating on the flaws.

CHAPTER 5

Can Self-Image Be Improved?

Building and maintaining a positive self-image and good self-esteem is a lifelong process. People are always capable of change, because new perceptions can be learned and new experiences can overcome old ones. An individual with low self-esteem, little self-confidence, or continual feelings of worthlessness and inadequacy can improve self-image and learn to be happier. Some people use self-help techniques, while others take advantage of professional counseling or therapy, but no one has to be stuck with distorted beliefs about self.

Self-Help to Improve Self-Image

The first step in improving self-image is realizing that beliefs acquired in the past do not accurately represent oneself and that perceptions can be questioned and eventually changed for the better. What was learned can be unlearned, and an unlovable self can become loved. When self-image reflects reality, self-esteem rises. One self-help approach, suggested by British psychiatrist Neel Burton, begins with taking inventory. People following this technique make two lists—one of their strengths and another of their achievements. Since those with low self-esteem often have trouble identifying their good points, Burton recommends getting a close friend or supportive family member to help make the lists. Once the lists are completed, the work is to read these lists every morning. At the same time, the person tries to practice thinking positively about himself or herself. Negative thoughts have to be questioned and banished. Burton explains, "Identify and challenge any negative thoughts about yourself such as 'I am a loser,' 'I never do anything right,' or 'No one really likes me.'"[40] Every time a person realizes such thoughts have crept in, he or she should substitute thinking positively about the self and affirm that he or she deserves to feel good.

During this time of improvement, it is vital to take especially good care of one's body and treat it as lovable and valuable. That means eating healthfully, showering, grooming, dressing in clean clothing, getting enough sleep, exercising appropriately, and even making one's physical living space clean and comfortable. Then, emotions and psychological needs must be cared for. Burton recommends spoiling oneself, doing at least one fun activity every day, and learning or completing one new activity, such as giving a party or taking music lessons. Finally, he suggests meeting social needs. He says, "Spend more time with those you hold near and dear. . . . Avoid people and places that treat you badly or make you feel bad about yourself."[41]

Burton's self-help procedures may sound simple, but they can be powerful methods for improving one's self-esteem. Other self-help experts offer similar recommendations for improving self-image and self-esteem. They are not complicated; they simply require the willingness to work and to change. Some people follow the guidance they find at reputable websites, such as those of major medical associations or government health agencies. Others use the support of family and friends along with their own determination to learn to love themselves. Some take classes online, at a community center, or at a college or join support groups in which people with self-esteem issues get together and encourage each other.

Still others turn to self-help books that emphasize building self-esteem and a positive self-image. Mandy overcame her self-image problems by beginning an extensive reading and learning program that included thirty books and following the advice she read that was most meaningful to her. She says that she went from "a weepy self-hating paralytically over-apologetic constantly worrying shy chick to a person who is quite the opposite." Today, as an adult who spent years overcoming her distorted thinking, she says, "If you met me in high school or college, you would not recognize me as the self-assured chick I am today. I owe it all to these 30 books."[42]

To improve self-image it is important to take care of one's body by getting enough exercise and being physically healthy, then emotions and psychological needs can be addressed.

No matter what the technique, all self-help guides emphasize learning to love and accept oneself. The British National Health Service explains that this means understanding that everyone is good at something and everyone has good points. People who find their own positive qualities and acknowledge them are learning to love themselves. It also means learning to be assertive and believing that everyone has the right to say no and to stand up for himself or herself. In addition, people with a poor self-image are extremely self-critical, especially about mistakes they make; instead, they must to learn to be kind to themselves. Psychiatrist Chris Williams explains, "Be compassionate to yourself. That means being gentle to yourself at times when you feel like being self-critical. Think what you'd say to a friend in a similar situation. We often give far better advice to others than we do to ourselves." He encourages, "You might have low confidence now because of what happened when you were growing up. But we can grow and develop new ways of seeing ourselves at any age."[43]

Talk Therapy to Improve Self-Image

Self-help programs can be beneficial, but for some people they are not enough. Many people need an objective person to help them identify and overcome negative thoughts and a poor self-image. For these people, psychological counseling or therapy can make a big difference in their lives. Carol, for example, sought help from psychotherapist Beverly Amsel when she was twenty-five years old. Carol was depressed and anxious much of the time. She told Amsel, "I am so unhappy. I look around and see other people my age having fun, loving their jobs, feeling good about themselves. I feel like such a nothing. I don't have a clue about what I want to be when I grow up. I'm scared to death when I go on a date that the guy will find me stupid and boring. I feel so awkward and uncomfortable around people."[44]

> **WORDS IN CONTEXT**
>
> **talk therapy**
>
> A treatment method that involves discussing mental and emotional issues to resolve psychological problems.

With her therapist, Carol explored her childhood experiences and how they had affected the development of her self-image and self-esteem. Carol's parents were divorced, and her father had limited involvement in her life. Her mother was career oriented and spent little time with her daughter. As an only child, Carol was alone a lot and made few friends in school. No one in her life showed much interest in her achievements, cared about her problems, or gave her the kind of praise that children crave. When Carol went to college, her parents decided that she would make a good lawyer and directed her to go to law school. Carol was not very excited about the career, but her parents told her she was foolish to reject their advice. They did not consider her feelings.

As a result of her experiences, Carol did not know who she was or what she wanted out of life. Amsel explains:

> For Carol, the emotional absence of her parents from her life, and the minimal appreciation and recognition they offered, contributed significantly to her inability to develop a separate self with feelings of value and confidence. Without the experience of parents responding to a child's spirit and achievements (whether taking first steps, laughing at their jokes, making a diorama, or going on a first date), children are deprived of the building blocks for self-confidence and self-esteem. To feel "I can do it," or even more important, "You are proud, pleased, and delighted with me," is a crucial experience that Carol never had.[45]

Over several months' time, Carol and Amsel talked through the anger and resentment Carol felt toward her parents, and the young woman decided to stop blaming them for her unhappiness and start taking charge of her life. With the therapist's encouragement, she began pushing herself to try new things and take some risks. She began dating, reached out for friendships, and took some college courses to help herself figure out the career path that interested her. She was anxious about the new experiences,

Psychological counseling can be helpful for people who are struggling to overcome negative thoughts and poor self-image. Having an objective person try to identify negative thoughts can be useful.

but she was also surprised and gratified by her successes. She grew in feelings of self-worth, self-esteem, and self-confidence. Supportive talk therapy made it possible for Carol to build a new self-image and think about herself in positive ways.

Self-Image and Cognitive Behavioral Therapy

Carol benefited from talk therapy and exploring the childhood issues that had distorted her self-image and harmed her self-esteem. Another form of therapy, known as cognitive behavioral therapy (CBT), has also been found to be extremely successful in helping people develop a positive self-image and good self-esteem. CBT is

Clothing and Self-Confidence

Several psychological studies have shown that the clothing people wear has a significant effect on their self-esteem and self-confidence and in the way others treat them. British psychologist Karen J. Pine explains, "When we put on a piece of clothing we cannot help but adopt some of the characteristics associated with it, even if we are unaware of it." That means people dressed in sloppy clothes may slouch and shuffle and feel unattractive, while people who are dressed up and in style feel powerful and good-looking. A person's feeling of self-confidence is appealing to other people, too. Those people are more likely to react with respect and enjoyment to a positive, smiling, confident individual. In 2014 the auto manufacturer Kia conducted a survey to find out which dressing and grooming practices make people feel confident. For men the top ten list included being freshly shaved, wearing a new suit, and splashing on a good aftershave. For women it was wearing a stylish black dress, high heels, and designer perfume. The clothes people choose to wear truly do affect the way they feel about themselves.

Quoted in Jill L. Ferguson, "How Clothing Choices Affect and Reflect Your Self-Image," *HuffPost* (blog), February 5, 2016. www.huffingtonpost.com.

a relatively short-term (five to ten months), goal-oriented, practical treatment method that focuses on understanding and changing present behaviors, thoughts, and feelings. It is an approach that is not concerned with figuring out the childhood causes of problems. Instead, CBT asks what can be done now to make the person more comfortable, happier, and better functioning. The goal is to give the person realistic and positive views about self and self-worth, and thus more control over his or her life. CBT emphasizes practical strategies for tackling problems and teaches clients the importance of fighting negative thoughts about self. Psychologist Ben Martin explains, "If our thoughts are too negative, it can block us seeing things or doing things that don't fit—that disconfirm— what we believe is true. In other words, we continue to hold on to the same old thoughts and fail to learn anything new."[46] Learning to question a poor self-image and to develop a new self-image becomes possible when negative thoughts are identified and rejected.

Kate was twenty-one years old and lived in Australia. She went to see a CBT counselor when her mother became worried about her unhappy feelings and inability to even try to look for a job. Kate was a shy, discouraged person with extremely low self-esteem. Much of her poor self-image was related to body image. Kate had struggled with weight issues all her life; during primary school and high school, other students teased her and called her "fatty." Her father also made negative comments about her body and pushed her to diet.

Kate had few friends growing up, but after graduation she began a relationship with a young man and started to feel better about herself. When her boyfriend broke up with her, however, she felt worse than ever and believed the cause of the rejection was her weight. At the time of her first counseling session, Kate related these negative experiences to the therapist and blamed her unhappiness on how fat and ugly she was.

At the end of their first meeting together, Kate's counselor concluded:

> At the moment Kate has such low self esteem that she doesn't even want to try to find a job, she thinks "who is ever going to hire me." Kate also described how her friends have stopped calling her because they say she is constantly criticising them. Kate stays at home all day and every time she looks in the mirror she thinks how ugly she is. It is important to note that Kate is currently within the healthy weight range for her age and height.[47]

The counselor understood that Kate's poor self-image developed from her early experiences in life, but in CBT the causes of a negative self-image are not important. Instead of talking about what happened in the past, the counselor organized the subsequent therapy sessions around Kate taking control of her life and setting goals for herself in the present. Kate decided she wanted to lose weight, improve her self-image and self-confidence, find a job, and improve her relationships with her friends.

Strategies That Modify Thinking

First the counselor offered some education, explaining that women are portrayed as extremely and unrealistically thin on television and in women's magazines. Kate read many women's magazines and usually felt worse after looking at them, so the counselor asked her to stop reading them altogether. Then the counselor gave Kate a practical homework assignment called Thought Stopping. The goal of Thought Stopping is to combat negative thinking. Every time Kate looked in the mirror, she was reinforcing her bad opinion of herself by thinking that she was ugly and fat. With the Thought Stopping technique, Kate had to recognize that she was having a negative thought and then say "stop" aloud. Next Kate had to say something positive about herself, such as "I'm a fit and healthy person" or "I'm honest and friendly."[48]

Kate worked conscientiously on the Thought Stopping exercise, but it was much harder than she expected. She was surprised to discover how frequently she had negative thoughts and how challenging it was to combat them. The counselor reassured her that these difficulties were normal and that it would take time to overcome her automatic negative thinking patterns. The counselor also suggested that Kate needed to get out in the world, enjoy some activity, and get her mind off herself. Kate had enjoyed sports in the past, so she agreed to join a netball club. (Netball is a game similar to basketball.) Both the physical activity and the socializing helped Kate feel better.

Then the counselor talked to Kate about how people with low self-esteem often criticize others to make themselves feel better and then lose those social contacts and feel worse than ever. Kate admitted that was what she had done with her friends. She agreed to get back in touch with them, tell them how much they meant to her, and practice saying positive things about them and about herself and her life. Over the course of several weeks of therapy, Kate's positive talk gradually became easier for her.

WORDS IN CONTEXT

positive talk

Self-talk, done either out loud or silently, that is used to give oneself encouragement and motivation.

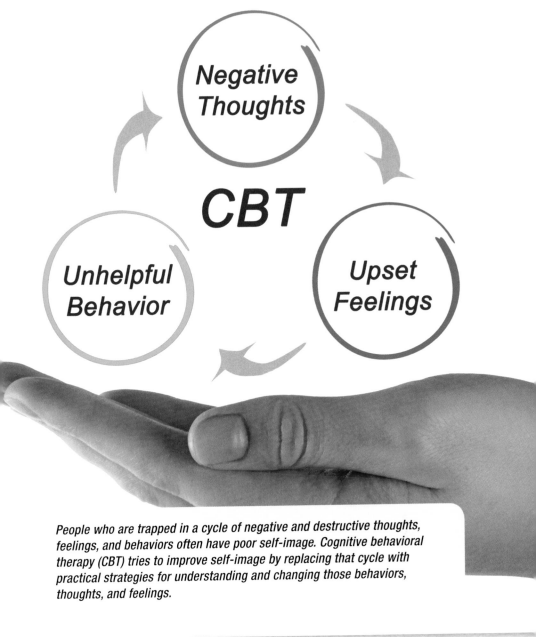

People who are trapped in a cycle of negative and destructive thoughts, feelings, and behaviors often have poor self-image. Cognitive behavioral therapy (CBT) tries to improve self-image by replacing that cycle with practical strategies for understanding and changing those behaviors, thoughts, and feelings.

Her friends came back into her life. They liked being around Kate again, and she started feeling more confident. She began going out and socializing regularly, and her self-esteem rose.

Finally, the counselor decided it was time to address the topic of employment. Kate confided that she had always wished to be a legal secretary. The counselor supported this goal and explained that mastering new skills would increase Kate's self-confidence even more and help her gain the courage to seek a job. Kate eagerly seized on this idea now that her self-image was becoming positive. She began teaching herself to type and enrolled in a secretarial course. Her life was now busy and happy, and Kate herself was optimistic about her future. At this point, Kate did not need counseling anymore. The counselor concluded, "Kate may still have a long road to travel in continuing to enhance her self esteem, however now she has more skills to help her on her way."[49] CBT is all about acquiring skills and practical techniques that enable a person to think accurately about self, leading to actions that will make a good self-image and positive self-esteem a reality.

Change Is Possible

Kate and Carol are not unusual people. Their stories are representative of what anybody can do who has the motivation to

Enjoy the Praise That Comes Your Way

Psychologist Guy Winch offers an easy tip for improving self-esteem: Learn to accept compliments and believe in them. Anyone can follow this advice. Winch explains:

> One of the trickiest aspects of improving self-esteem is that when we feel bad about ourselves we tend to be more resistant to compliments—even though that is when we most need them. So, set yourself the goal to tolerate compliments when you receive them, even if they make you uncomfortable (and they will). The best way to avoid the reflexive reactions of batting away compliments is to prepare simple set responses and train yourself to use them automatically whenever you get good feedback (e.g., "Thank you" or "How kind of you to say"). In time, the impulse to deny or rebuff compliments will fade—which will also be a nice indication your self-esteem is getting stronger.

Guy Winch, "5 Ways to Build Lasting Self-Esteem," Ideas.TED.com, August 23, 2016. http://ideas.ted.com.

improve self-image and enhance self-esteem. As psychologists, psychiatrists, and counselors say over and over, self-image is learned. The false beliefs upon which a poor self-image is based can be eliminated. No one deserves to live with a negative self-image and low self-esteem. Darlene Lancer, a marriage and family therapist, had to battle her own very low self-esteem before she could use her experience of healing herself to help others. She says, "The most important belief is . . . that you can change. . . . Your mind is a powerful, creative gift. Learn to use it to work for you, not against you."[50] Anyone can learn to recognize and value the good and positive in themselves and to respect the amazing, worthwhile individual that one is.

SOURCE NOTES

Introduction: What Is Self-Image?

1. Roy F. Baumeister, *The Self in Social Psychology*. Philadelphia: Psychology Press, 1999, p. 5.
2. Roy F. Baumeister and Brad Bushman, *Social Psychology and Human Nature: Brief Version*. Belmont, CA: Thomson Wadsworth, 2008, p. viii.

Chapter 1: How Does Self-Image Develop?

3. Quoted in J. Gavin Bremner and Theodore D. Wachs, eds., *The Wiley-Blackwell Handbook of Infant Development*, 2nd ed. West Sussex, UK: Blackwell, 2010, p. 324.
4. Quoted in Jaine Strauss and George R. Goethals, eds., *The Self: Interdisciplinary Approaches*. New York: Springer, 1991, p. 123.
5. Quoted in Molly McElroy, "Children's Self-Esteem Already Established by Age 5, New Study Finds," UW Today, University of Washington, November 2, 2015. www.washington.edu.
6. Quoted in McElroy, "Children's Self-Esteem Already Established by Age 5, New Study Finds."
7. David Dean Witt, "Notes for Emotional Development, the Self and Identity," School of Family and Consumer Sciences, University of Akron. www3.uakron.edu.
8. Quoted in Dan G. Blazer, *The Age of Melancholy: "Major Depression" and Its Social Origin*. New York: Routledge, 2005, p. 142.
9. Tanja G. Baudson et al., "More than Only Skin Deep: Appearance Self-Concept Predicts Most of Secondary School Students' Self-Esteem," *Frontiers in Psychology*, October 18, 2016. http://journal.frontiersin.org.
10. David H. Demo, "The Self-Concept over Time: Research Issues and Directions," *Annual Review of Sociology*, vol. 18, 1992, p. 316.

11. Demo, "The Self-Concept over Time," p. 311.
12. Demo, "The Self-Concept over Time," p. 323.

Chapter 2: Positive Self-Image and High Self-Esteem

13. Charles Stangor, *Principles of Social Psychology*. Victoria, BC: BC Open Textbook Collection, 2014, p. 135.
14. Stangor, *Principles of Social Psychology*, p. 118.
15. UC-Davis Health Center, "Self-Esteem." www.ucdmc.uc davis.edu.
16. Witt, "Notes for Emotional Development, the Self and Identity."
17. Nathaniel Branden, "Your Role in Your Child's Self-Esteem," Nathaniel Branden, 2013. www.nathanielbranden.com.
18. KidsHealth, "Developing Your Child's Self-Esteem," September 2016. http://kidshealth.org.
19. Stangor, *Principles of Social Psychology*, p. 135.
20. Stangor, *Principles of Social Psychology*, p. 138.
21. Stangor, *Principles of Social Psychology*, p. 141.

Chapter 3: Negative Self-Image and Low Self-Esteem

22. Baumeister and Bushman, *Social Psychology and Human Nature*, p. 102.
23. Quoted in NHS Choices, "Raising Low Self-Esteem," March 31, 2017. www.nhs.uk.
24. Ronald Mah, "Building Self-Esteem in the Adult-Child System," Ronald Mah, 2007. www.ronaldmah.com.
25. Quoted in Preston Ni, "10 Signs of a Narcissistic Parent," *Communication Success* (blog), *Psychology Today*, February 28, 2016. www.psychologytoday.com.
26. Quoted in Margarita Tartakovsky, "10 Strategies for Helping Kids with ADHD Build Self-Confidence," *World of Psychology* (blog), Psych Central, January 2, 2014. https://psychcentral.com.
27. Quoted in Patricia Quinn, "'I'm Way Too Hard on Myself,'" *ADDitude*, Summer 2012. www.additudemag.com.

28. Ryan J. Voigt, "Who Me? Self-Esteem for People with Disabilities," brainline.org, 2009. www.brainline.org.
29. Quoted in Margie Warrell, "For Women to Rise We Must Close 'the Confidence Gap,'" *Forbes*, January 20, 2016. www.forbes.com.

Chapter 4: What About Body Image?

30. Susan Paxton, "Childhood Trends in Body Image," Kids-Matter. www.kidsmatter.edu.au.
31. Paxton, "Childhood Trends in Body Image."
32. Quoted in Jonathan Wells, "Are Action Figures Giving Boys Body-Image Anxiety?," *Telegraph* (London), September 17, 2015. www.telegraph.co.uk.
33. Baudson et al., "More than Only Skin Deep."
34. Thomas Holbrook, "One Man's Battle with Anorexia," *NOVA*, PBS, December 1, 2000. www.pbs.org.
35. Holbrook, "One Man's Battle with Anorexia."
36. Holbrook, "One Man's Battle with Anorexia."
37. Courtney, "Courtney's Story," Eating Disorders in a Disordered Culture. http://eating.ucdavis.edu.
38. Courtney, "Courtney's Story."
39. Quoted in Mackenzie Wagoner, "6 Times Jennifer Lawrence Took a Stand on Body Positivity," *Vogue*, April 7, 2016. www.vogue.com.

Chapter 5: Can Self-Image Be Improved?

40. Neel Burton, "Building Confidence and Self-Esteem," *Hide and Seek* (blog), *Psychology Today*, May 30, 2012. www.psychologytoday.com.
41. Burton, "Building Confidence and Self-Esteem."
42. Mandy, "30 Self-Help Books That Permanently Changed My Life," *xoJane*, February 19, 2013. www.xojane.com.
43. Quoted in NHS Choices, "Raising Low Self-Esteem."
44. Quoted in Beverly Amsel, "The Effects of Parental Involvement on Self-Confidence and Self-Esteem," Good Therapy.org, July 16, 2013. www.goodtherapy.org.

45. Amsel, "The Effects of Parental Involvement on Self-Confidence and Self-Esteem."

46. Ben Martin, "In-Depth: Cognitive Behavioral Therapy," Psych Central, May 17, 2016. https://psychcentral.com.

47. Australian Institute of Professional Counsellors, "A Case of Low Self Esteem," *Counselling Connection* (blog), May 3, 2007. www.counsellingconnection.com.

48. Australian Institute of Professional Counsellors, "A Case of Low Self Esteem."

49. Australian Institute of Professional Counsellors, "A Case of Low Self Esteem."

50. Darlene Lancer, "Low Self-Esteem Is Learned," Psych Central, May 17, 2016. https://psychcentral.com.

Books

Karen Bluth, *The Self-Compassion Workbook for Teens: Mindfulness and Compassion Skills to Overcome Self-Criticism and Embrace Who You Are*. Oakland, CA: Instant Help, 2017.

Shari Brady, *It's Not What You're Eating, It's What's Eating You: A Teenager's Guide to Preventing Eating Disorders and Loving Yourself*. New York: Skyhorse, 2017.

Meghan Green and J.R. Lankford, *Body Image and Body Shaming*. Farmington Hills, MI: Lucent, 2017.

Viola Jones and Edward Willett, *Conquering Negative Body Image*. New York: Rosen, 2016.

Wendy L. Moss and Donald A. Moses, *The Tween Book: A Growing-Up Guide for the Changing You*. Washington, DC: Magination, 2015.

Lisa M. Schab, *The Self-Esteem Habit for Teens: 50 Simple Ways to Build Your Confidence Every Day*. Oakland, CA: Instant Help, 2018.

Internet Sources

Child and Youth Health: Teen Health, "Self-Esteem and Confidence," June 27, 2016. www.cyh.com/HealthTopics/HealthTopic Details.aspx?id=2161&np=293&p=243.

KidsHealth, "How's Your Self-Esteem?" http://kidshealth.org/en /teens/self-esteem-quiz.html.

Websites

About-Face (www.about-face.org). This organization's goal is to expose and stand up against the media messages that harm self-esteem and body image in women and girls.

National Association for Self Esteem (http://healthyselfesteem .org). Visitors to this site can take a guided tour to explore their level of self-esteem, learn to boost self-esteem through interactive activities, and read about what self-esteem is and why it matters.

National Eating Disorders Association (www.nationaleating disorders.org). For people of all ages, the National Eating Disorders Association offers education about eating disorders and their causes, a discussion of body image, a help line, and stories about support and recovery.

ReachOut.com (http://au.reachout.com). This large Australian website is specifically designed for young people to help them with the variety of difficult issues they may face as they mature. Emotional and psychological issues addressed include bullying, depression, social relationships, and personal identity.

INDEX

Note: Boldface page numbers indicate illustrations.

adolescence, self-image and, 15–16

American Psychiatric Association, 46

American Psychological Association, 42, 55

Amsel, Beverly, 59, 60

animals, self-awareness in, 13

anorexia nervosa, 50, 52, **53**

definition of, 50

anxiety disorder

definition of, 37

attention-deficit/hyperactivity disorder (ADHD), 39

Baghurst, Timothy, 47

Baumeister, Roy F., 6, 8, 34

Bleidorn, Wiebke, 42–43

body dysmorphic disorder (BDD), 51

body image

definition of, 44

effects of unrealistic body-type standards on, 46–47, **48**, 55

impacts of serious disease on, 54

importance of, 49–50

negative, eating disorders and, 50–55, **53**

unachievable/unrealistic body types, 46–47, **48**

brain, areas/functions of, **4**

Branden, Nathaniel, 27

British National Health Service, 59

bulimia, 50, 53–55

definition of, 52

Burton, Neel, 56–57

Bushman, Brad, 8, 34

Carey, Mariah, 42

clothing/grooming practices, self-confidence and, 62

cognition, definition of, 19

cognitive behavioral therapy (CBT), 61–63

Common Sense Media, 47

compliments, learning to accept, 66

culture, self-esteem and, 40–41

Cvencek, Dario, 14, 15

DeCasper, Anthony J., 9

Demo, David H., 19

depression, 32, 35, 52, 54

definition of, 35

disability, self-esteem and, 39–40, **41**, 43

disability/disease
  adjusting to changes associated with, 54
  self-esteem and, 39–40, **41**

eating disorders, 50–54
  in males, 51–52
the elderly, self-esteem in, 25
Erikson, Erik, 16–17
explicit, definition of, 10

Fifer, William P., 9

Gallup, Gordon G., Jr., 12, 13
gender/gender identity
  in children with high self-esteem, 15
  self-esteem and, 42–43
Greenwald, Anthony, 15
grooming practices/clothing, self-confidence and, 62

Holbrook, Thomas, 51–52

ideal self, 7–8
  conflict between actual self and, 21–22
  definition of, 8
implicit, definition of, 10

infants, development of body awareness in, 9–10

Lancer, Darlene, 67
Lawrence, Jennifer, 55

Mah, Ronald, 36–37
Martin, Ben, 62
Mate, Gabor, 39
Matlen, Terry, 39
men/boys
  eating disorders in, 51–53
  grooming/dressing and self-esteem in, 62
  unrealistic body-type standards and body image in, 47
mirror recognition, 10–12, 13

narcissism, 31
  definition of, 31
  in parents, impacts on child's self-esteem, 37–38
negative feelings/thoughts
  CBT and strategies for fighting, 62–63
  cycle of, self-image and, **65**
  psychological counseling for, 59–61
  self-help to combat, 56–59

Ni, Preston, 38

opinion polls. *See* surveys

parents
  children's body image and,
    47
  development of self-
    esteem and, 25–27,
    35–38
  emotionally absent, 60
  narcissistic, 37–38
  overly critical, 35–37
  role in development of
    child's self-image, 12
  teens' communication
    with, 36
Paxton, Susan, 45
perception(s)
  about self
    body image and, 44
    possibility of changing,
      56
    self-image and, 18
    view of ideal self and, 20
  definition of, 15
  distorted, of body, 51
personality traits, as
  component of self-image,
  5, 6
physical description, as
  component of self-image,
  5
Pine, Karen J., 62

polls. *See* surveys
positive talk, 64–65
  definition of, 64

Rochat, Philippe, 10

schema, definition of, 6
self-awareness
  among animals, 13
  beginnings of, 9
  explicit *vs.* implicit, 10
self-complexity, 23–24
  definition of, 23
self-confidence
  clothing/grooming
    practices and, 62
  feelings of inadequacy
    and, 32
  low self-esteem and, 33
  self-image and, 19, 50
  significance of self in, 8
  therapy and, 65–66
self-conscious/self-
  consciousness, 18–19,
  32
  definition of, 33
self-esteem, 6–7
  age at establishment of,
    14
  culture and, 40–41
  definition of, 20
  in the elderly, 25
  gender and, 42–43

   benefits of, 24–25
   maintaining, 28–31
   impact of body image on,
      49–50
low
   causes of, 35–38
   characteristics of people
      with, 32–33
   disadvantages of, 34–35
   possibility of improving,
      43, 66–67
   success/fame and, 42
   test of, 30
self-help, 56–59
   definition of, 57
self-identity, 21–23, 32
   definition of, 21
self-image
   adolescence and, 15–16
   changes over lifetime in,
      19
   in children, 12–15
   components of, 5–6
   cycle of negative feelings
      and, **65**
   definition of, 5
   influences on, 5
   negative, cognitive
      behavioral therapy for,
      61–63
   parents' role in
      development of, 12

possibility of improving,
   43
   self-help and, 56–59
self-knowledge
   in infants, 9–10
   self-complexity and,
      23–24
self-schemas, 6
social roles, as component
   of self-image, 5–6
Stangor, Charles, 21–22,
   23, 28, 31
subjective, definition of, 45
surveys
   on grooming practices
      and feelings of
      confidence, 62
   of teen girls on comparing
      their bodies with
      celebrities' bodies, 48

talk therapy, 59–61
   definition of, 59
teenagers
   body image and, 47–49
   causes of low self-esteem
      in, 36
   identity crisis in, 16–17
Thought Stopping, 64
Tye, Kristine, 36

University of California–Davis
   Health Center, 24–25

Voigt, Ryan J., 40

Williams, Chris, 35, 59
Williams, Serena, 42
Winch, Guy, 66
Winslet, Kate, 42
Witt, David Dean, 16, 25

women/girls
    grooming/dressing and self-
      esteem in, 62
    self-esteem among, 42–43
    unrealistic body-type
      standards and body image
      in, 46–47, **48**, 55, 64

PICTURE CREDITS

Cover: Thinkstock Images/iStock

4: Maury Aaseng

7: Shutterstock/Rawpixel

11: Thinkstock Images/iStock

14: Depositphotos/Monkey Business

18: iStockphoto.com/Antonio Diaz

22: iStockphoto/asiseeit

26: Shutterstock.com/Filimonov

29: Shutterstock/CLS Digital Arts

34: Thinkstock Images/iStock

38: Shutterstock.com/Lopolo

41: iStockphoto.com/Ron Bailey

46: iStockphoto/mactrunk

48: Depositphotos/konradbak

53: iStockphoto.com/People Images

58: Shutterstock/Jacek Chabraszewski

61: iStockphoto/Clark and Company

65: Depositphotos/vaeenma

ABOUT THE AUTHOR

Toney Allman holds a BS in psychology from Ohio State University and an MA in clinical psychology from the University of Hawaii. She currently lives in Virginia, where she enjoys a rural lifestyle and researching and writing about a variety of topics for students.